IØ118473

Endorsements and Praise
for the
Maxwell Winston Stone Books

...Carwile's first novel should have a place in most book collections, with crossover appeal for readers who enjoyed Mitch Album's The Five People You Meet in Heaven.

—*The Library Journal*

Thank you very much for your book on "Attitude." It was 100% good stuff that we all need to absorb...

—Steve Spurrier, Head Football Coach
University of South Carolina

[In the hospital] the view for us all changes depending whether we are looking up from the gurney...or a doctor gazing down. The Maxwell Winston Stone Series *helps to remind us all of the journey and the big picture.*

—Douglas V. Mayeda, MD,
Diplomat of the American
Board of Emergency Medicine

I have always taught my children to look on the bright side of life—and [your book] **Attitude** *expresses this concept perfectly.*

—Bill Owens
Governor of Colorado, 1999-2007

These books speak to the world. Everyone should read them.

—Edwin Alexander
Former Director of
The Federal Home Loan Bank

Thank you for your book on **Attitude***. I'm adding it to my personal lending library at the office so my staff and others can read it, too.*

—Jennifer Granholm
Governor of Michigan

One of the most spiritual yet realistic books of our time—they're phenomenal.

—Dr. Robert Carrol
Radiology Medicine

CRÈME
de la
CRÈME

**132 Greatest Stories
and Quotes for**

Speakers, Seekers

and Writers

Ernie Carwile

CRÈME de la CRÈME

132 Greatest Stories and Quotes for

Speakers, Seekers

and Writers

Ernie Carwile

Verbena Pond Publishing Co., LLC

For information, contact 303-641-8632.

ISBN: 978-0-9796176-9-0

Library of Congress Control Number: 2015914063

Printed in the United States

Other Books by Ernie Carwile

The Magic of Creativity

And the Animals Shall Teach Us: Angels in Disguise

Attitude: It's Not What You See, It's How You See

Connected By The Soul: Oh, The Oneness of Us All

Reclaiming the Power of Silence

Persistence: The Art of Failing Until You Succeed

Where Do We Go From Here?
Death, The Next Great Adventure

Never Good Enough:
Discover the Treasure of Self-Acceptance

Chipped But Not Broken 2:
When Adversity Enhances The Human Spirit

The Storyteller 1

TABLE OF CONTENTS

THE CRÈME de la CRÈME

As a speaker and writer myself, I have spent the past thirty-five years both writing and gathering great, great stories and quotes to utilize in my own speaking engagements and book-writing.

Why? Because I recognized early on that the best speakers throughout time always employed stories to convey their messages. If a picture says a thousand words, it could be argued that a powerful story communicates an idea not only through visual or spoken words but more importantly they also speak directly to the heart. Former Presidents John F. Kennedy, Abraham Lincoln and Ronald Reagan, along with Aristotle, Confucius, Mark Twain and Will Rogers all utilized storytelling in their writing and speeches.

The three types of stories most used are parables, anecdotes and fables. Similar, they are quite alike in that they all convey powerful or meaningful messages, some that are quite stunning; yet there are also differences. For example, parables, on one hand, are sometimes called soul stories because they speak directly to the heart, meaning you may not be able to understand them through logic, or using the left-side of the brain.

Where anecdotal stories are normally true, meaning they actually happened, parables and fables are not necessarily true but convey a lesson or message so meaningful that the veracity of the story—whether it actually happened or not—becomes insignificant.

The following pages are filled with one hundred and thirty-two anecdotal/parable/fable stories and quotes—the crème-de-la-crème. They are disclosed in twenty different topics, each numbered accordingly. Also, keep in mind that many of the stories and quotes can be simply altered with a few word changes to allow them to be used in different topics or categories.

If you have any other stories you have discovered/written and would like to share, feel free to email them to: carwile64@gmail.com.

For those who may wish to learn more about Maxwell Winston Stone, go to www.ErnieCarwile.com and order the book, *The Storyteller.*

Good reading!

Ernie Carwile

Author and Creator of
The MAXWELL WINSTON STONE Series

www.ErnieCarwile.com
carwile64@gmail.com
303-641-8632

PROLOGUE

There's an odd story I once read; I think it was about a couple of Hindu fellows, one a teacher—a really smart yogi—and the other a student. They were out in this field, the teacher standing, the student sitting on the ground, leaning against a tree. The student confessed one of the biggest obstacles to his growth was a desire to experience having a wife and children.

His teacher looked upon his young, brilliant student and, rather than urging him to lose this dream, instead told him to close his eyes and concentrate on feeling the sun's relaxing rays shine upon his face. It was a beautiful day, and the sun's warmth spread across his body bringing drowsiness, until he soon fell asleep, his teacher standing before him.

Suddenly the young man jolted awake to the

sound of thunder and rain pouring down upon him. Jumping up, he looked for his teacher, but instead saw a great flood bearing down upon him. Unable to do anything, the young man was swept up in a wild, powerful flood that carried him away for a long, long time.

Constantly struggling to keep his head above the water, he eventually saw a house with people standing on the roof. Swimming toward the roof, he held out an arm in hopes they could grab him. As fate had it, a man did just that, grabbed his arm and pulled him up out of the flood's dangerous current. Catching his breath, the young man thanked the older man who'd saved him and then noticed there were also an older woman and a beautiful young girl, prob- ably, he thought, their daughter.

After the flood receded, the older man invited the younger man to stay with them. He told him they could feed him and give him a room if he would help them clean up. Having nothing better to do, he agreed.

As it happened, they all soon became friends—

weeks turned into months, and the boy helped with planting the crops and became indispensable with the other farm chores. He and the daughter also grew very fond of one another until a marriage was agreed upon.

Life was good for them all; the young couple produced two wonderful children, a girl and boy. Eventually the parents passed on; the couple inherited the farm and became even more prosperous. The man achieved everything he wanted: a wife, children, farm, property, happiness, everything.

Until one day, a torrential rain came suddenly, followed by a huge flood. The man quickly ran to save his children, only to arrive just as the floodwaters sucked them under.

Looking next for his wife, he saw the flood take her.

Destroyed, grieved beyond all hope, he fell to the ground in anguish and was also swept away by the flood.

The next thing the young man realized upon

opening his eyes was the astonishing fact he was sitting in the original field, leaning against the same tree as before, his face warmed by the sun, his teacher standing before him smiling.

Bewildered and confused, he pleaded for an explanation.

Mischievously his teacher challenged, "Now, you tell me. Which experience is more real: the dream you just had, or the reality of us talking in this field?"

Perplexed, the young man had no answer.

I. Acceptance

1 "Most every human craves to be accepted; not so much in what they show others on the outside—the masks they wear—but who they really are on the inside."

—John Powell 1925-2009)
Jesuit Priest and author of
Why Am I Afraid To Show You Who I Am?

2 Here is a heartwarming story that came out of the Vietnam War.

He was assigned to Vietnam right after his wife became pregnant with their first child. Just after his arrival in the foreign jungle, two tragic things happened. First, he stepped on a land mine and lost both legs and an arm; then, he was captured and became a prisoner for five years. During these terrible years, his wife had given birth to their son, who had grown from a baby to a little boy just starting kindergarten.

When the POW's were finally released and flown back to the U.S., there were actually two planes involved. One carried the healthier men who received all the media attention, while the other plane held the men who had been badly injured. These men were quietly taken off from the backside of the second plane.

Meeting the second plane were the wife and five-year-old son. The young boy was both nervous and excited as he'd never seen his dad in person before. Closely observing as his dad was taken off the plane, he noticed his dad didn't have any legs. Turning to his mother he whispered, "Mommy, Daddy doesn't have any legs, does he?"

His mother, trying to be strong though tears were running down her face replied, "No, sweetie, he doesn't."

As the men wheeled his father closer, the little boy saw his dad was missing an arm, too. "Mommy," he whispered, "Daddy doesn't have an arm either, does he?" His mother shook her head no, barely able to keep from bursting into tears.

After a long pause in which you could tell the boy was thinking really hard, he turned to his mom and said a beautiful thing. Leaning over he whispered, "Let's not tell him."

3 "Oh Great Spirit, grant that I may never judge another until I have walked a mile in his [or her] moccasins."

—Old Indian Proverb

4 Here is a true story a school teacher shared with me.

A mother-in-law volunteered to work one Sunday in the nursery school. As fate would have it, the opening she filled was the classroom her grandson attended.

After a very, very difficult time mainly because of her three-year old grandson's bossiness towards the other kids, she leaned over to the other teacher and whispered, "You know, any other kid and I'd call him a bully, but since he's my grandson, I'll just say he has leadership potential."

5 "No one knows another person's burden."

—Maxwell Winston Stone

6 A Jackie Robinson Story

Most people today know that Jackie Robinson was the first black major league baseball player when Branch Rickey, owner of the Brooklyn Dodgers, signed him to play in 1947. Rickey and Robinson openly talked about the difficulties Robinson would face—the prejudice he would experience.

From baseball history, we know that Jackie did experience gut-wrenching prejudice. Perhaps the worst case came when he was dealing with enormous heckling from the crowd after making a critical error that allowed a runner to score. As the fans booed even louder, Jackie made another error and it seemed a riot was going to occur.

It was then that Peewee Reese, the Dodger's outstanding shortstop came over and in front of the crowded stadium simply placed his arm around Jackie's shoulder until the crowd quieted down. Jackie then went on to play a suburb game.

Reflecting back, Jackie later said that Reese's simple act saved his career. "Pee Wee made me feel accepted, like I belonged. It made all the difference in my career."

II. ADVERSITY—
CHIPPED BUT
NOT BROKEN

7 "Adversity has the effect of eliciting talents which, in prosperous circumstances, would have lain dormant."

—Horace (65 BC-8 BC)

8 **True Story**

In Ireland, following the potato famine, when economic struggles were the norm of the day, one large Irish family decided they had to get to America to find a better way of life. The father agreed to stop drinking at the pubs and started working three jobs; the four boys worked wherever they could find odd jobs while the three girls and mother sold butter and eggs, and did laundry and housekeeping jobs for the richer families. All the money the family accumulated went towards one goal—paying the cost of tickets for a boat ride that would carry them to the United States of America and a better life.

The hard work by the entire family paid

off as they finally saved up enough money. However, when buying the ticket, the father discovered they had only earned enough money to buy non-refundable tickets. After assuring himself that nothing could stop them from going; he paid all the money his family had saved. Plans were made to take a ship that was leaving in only two weeks.

Then one of the sons was bitten by a rabid dog. At first they assured themselves this would not affect them leaving, that is until a veterinarian informed them the boy would have to be quarantined for four weeks. Stunned over this unexpected adversity; all their dreams dashed in a split second, the family was devastated.

The father was especially embittered, basically at God for causing the huge setback, and began drinking up any money they had while constantly cursing God.

However, upon entering a pub one afternoon, he overheard some men talking about how an American ship had sunk after hitting an iceberg, killing over fifteen hundred people. With chills running down his spine, he asked the name of the ship. When he heard "the Titanic" he nearly fainted for that was the exact ship they were booked to sail on.

Running home, he gathered the family and shared the news. They got down on their knees and thanked God for saving their lives. All knelt in wonder over what, initially had seemed the worst thing, but proved to be the greatest blessing of all.

9 "Adversity introduces a person to themselves."

—Maxwell Winston Stone

10 Stradivarius Violins

Remember that the famed Stradivarius violin, perhaps the greatest violin ever made, was harvested from only the toughest forest in Northern Croatia. This durable wood, known for its extreme density, resulted in slow growth brought about by the harshest winds and weather conditions in the frigid Croatian winters.

Why did the violin maker use such wood?

Because only the toughest wood, wood that had been grown under the most adverse circumstances, could produce the sweetest sounds in the world.

Could this be the same for you and me?

11 "Every person must walk through their 'fire' alone. This is what gives us our character and strength."

—Maxwell Winston Stone

12 The Butterfly Story

As a kid, did you ever watch a butterfly squirming and struggling to get itself out of the cocoon it had been growing in?

It is actually a frustrating and painful process to observe the incredible effort the butterfly expends to finally squeeze itself out of the tight cocoon.

Watching this, you might even be tempted to want to help the poor butterfly out by cutting open the cocoon, BUT DON'T.

Why? Because it is precisely this act of struggling out of the cocoon which actually saves its life. You see the struggle is nature's way of insuring that blood from the creature's body is pushed into the wings which is necessary for the butterfly to be able to fly. Without this struggle, this adversity of having to painfully squeeze and squirm out of the cocoon, the butterfly would be flightless.

This is the same for us; the adversities in our lives are there for a purpose, a reason, a way to teach us something we need to learn.

For more stories on adversity, go to www.ErnieCarwile.com and order the book, *Chipped But Not Broken*.

III. APPRECIATION

13 "Thanksgiving is one of the avenues through which the soul finds a larger field of expression."

—Charles Fillmore (1854-1948)
Cofounder of Unity

14 This is a poem written anonymously by a Confederate soldier. It allows us to recognize how we can learn to be appreciative for all the things that life presents us:

> I asked God for strength, that I might achieve,
> I was made weak, that I might learn to humbly obey.
> I asked for health, that I might do greater things,
> I was given infirmity, that I might do better things.
>
> I asked for riches, that I might be happy,
> I was given poverty, that I might be wise.
> I asked for power, that I might have the praise of men,
> I was given weakness, that I might feel the need of God.

CRÈME de la CRÈME

I asked for all things, that I might enjoy
life,
I was given life, that I might enjoy all
things.

I got nothing that I asked for—but
everything I had hoped for.
Almost despite myself, my unspoken
prayers were answered.
I am, among all men, most richly blessed.

15 "Life is a blessing or a curse, according to
how we see it."

—Maxwell Winston Stone

16 It has been said that the most exceptional
asset of Alberto Giacometti, the famous Swiss
sculptor, was that he used only four models
in sculpting his hundreds of artwork: his
wife, his sister and two close friends—just
these four!

When asked why, he jubilantly responded, "These four are enough. You see, my joy comes from looking at the same face every day and seeing what's new...what has changed. Every morning when I awake, I look at my wife, smile and say, 'Thank you God for the new beauty before me and for the fresh spirit I see in her each day.'"

You see none of us are the same people we were the day before, and perhaps only by integrating a sense of appreciation can we then see all the beauty this world holds.

17 "If the only prayer you ever say in your entire life is, 'Thank You,' it will be enough."

—Meister Eckhart (1260-1328)
Theologian, Mystic

18 From the famous composer Joseph Hayden, we can learn how he displayed the importance of having a sense of appreciation in a most unique way.

When asked how he created such beautiful music, he said, "Whenever I am ready to begin composing a new symphony, I first close my eyes, pray and then give thanks to God that I have already completed it."

The bewildered person stuttered, "You mean you give thanks for something you haven't even received yet?"

"Oh yes," replied the composer, "this insures that I will receive a great piece of music."

IV. ATTITUDE—
IT's NOT WHAT YOU SEE, IT's HOW YOU SEE

19 "Attitude is a choice. It is something you decide upon ahead of time...it's how you arrange your thoughts that counts."

—Maxwell Winston Stone

20 Two Shoe Salesmen

There was an experienced salesman who was sent by his company to see if a new market could be opened up in Africa. The company manufactured shoes and already had stores throughout the world, but none in Africa.

Most anxious to hear from the salesman; they waited and waited. After what seemed a reasonable time and still hearing nothing, they began to worry: Was he hurt? Did he even arrive?

After four worry-filled weeks, they finally received a telegram: "Coming home on the next plane. Hopeless market. *No one here wears shoes.*"

Greatly disappointed over the experienced salesman's feedback, they almost dropped the idea for an African market...until someone suggested they try again with a relatively new salesman; and so they did and waited.

Like before, they heard nothing for week after week. Finally, after the fourth week they received his telegram, though this time it read: "Fantastic market. Have mailed over 800 orders. Unlimited market here. You see, *no one here wears shoes!*"

Same place/circumstances but different perspective can make a huge difference.

❦

21 "We don't see things as they are; we see things as we are."

—Anais Nin (1914-1977)
Author

22 Can you remember who invented the first steam boat?

It was Robert Fulton, but what you don't know was the reaction of the people who were standing on the shore watching to see if it would work. *The Clermont*, the ship's name, started spewing out sparks as it built up steam. Negative and pessimistic about this new-fangled contraption, they screamed, "It'll never go. It'll never go."

Of course it did and the large ship began moving up the river; and in doing so, it radically changed the shipping industry. But the second invaluable thing to remember is what those same negative people watching from the shore yelled out next. After recovering from the shock of it actually moving forward, they next screamed, "It'll never stop. It'll never stop."

23 "Whether you believe you can do a thing, or not do it, you are right."

—Henry Ford (1863-1947)
American Industrialist

24 If we are fortunate, sometimes our negative attitudes will be reflected back to us so we can see how foolish we've been.

In the early 1900s, a bishop was invited to meet with a college president and faculty of the physics department. During the meeting, the president asked the learned bishop to speculate on future advancements in technology, especially in the area of man learning to fly.

Arrogantly, the bishop orated, "Man will never fly. Why, if God wanted us to fly he would have given us wings."

The key missing ingredient here is that the bishop was from Dayton, Ohio and his last name just happened to be W-R-I-G-H-T.

Even more fascinating is that, in just a few years, it would be his two sons, Wilbur and Orville, who would be the first persons to fly a plane at Kitty Hawk.

For more stories on attitude, go to www.ErnieCarwile.com and order the book, *It's Not WHAT You See, But HOW You See.*

V. On the Necessity of Change

25 "The mind stretched by a new idea can never return to its original dimension."

—Oliver Wendell Holmes (1841-1935)
American Justice of the Supreme Court

26 Training Fleas

Did you know that fleas can be trained to jump to only a specific height? It's true. Fleas can be trained by putting them into a box that has a lid on it. As the fleas jump up and hit the lid they get a headache (or whatever a flea gets from getting bonked on the head) and will soon learn to jump only high enough not to hit the lid. Eventually you can even take off the lid and the fleas will not jump out. Either they have learned or been conditioned to jump only so high.

Now ask yourself this: "In what ways have I trained myself to limit what I can accomplish? What beliefs or conditioning governing my life keeps me from releasing my greater potential?"

27 "God, grant me the serenity to accept the things I cannot change; the courage to change the things I can; and the wisdom to know the difference."

—Reinhold Niebuhr (1892-1971)
American Theologian

28 The Lobster Story

Once upon a time, when the world had just been created, there was a lobster that was sure the Creator made a mistake when designing his shell. You see, the lobster grew and became bigger than his shell, causing him great pain. To the Creator, he entreated: "I wish to make a complaint. I have discovered You must have made a mistake. It seems that, just when my shell begins to fit properly, I have to shed my old shell for a new one."

To his complaint, the Creator responded: "But that is the exact way I designed it to be—by giving up the old, smaller shell, you would be able to grow."

"Oh, I understand that," said the lobster, "but I don't want to change. I'd rather stay the way I am."

"Are you sure that's what you really want?" the Creator asked.

"Yes, yes," said the lobster and the Creator granted his wish.

Greatly pleased now, the lobster often commented how much he liked his old shell...until it became too tight and uncomfortable because of his normal growth. Eventually, it became so tight the lobster had trouble breathing. Gasping as he returned to the Creator he exclaimed, "It seems you've made another mistake for my shell keeps shrinking."

"Oh no," said the Creator, "Your shell hasn't shrunk, what has happened is that you have grown—you've changed—which is why your shell no longer fits."

Thinking about the information the Creator just presented him, he suddenly exclaimed, "You designed me to lose my shell so I could grow into a new and bigger one."

"Yes," responded the Creator, "this is how it is for all living things. You see, this is why each of you must let go of old parts of yourself so that you can become bigger and better; otherwise, you won't be able to breathe and you will die."

29 "If you always do what you always did, you'll always get what you always got."

—Attributed to Oprah Winfrey

30 Wise old King Solomon gave us these words.

For everything there is a season:

a time to be born, a time to die,

a time to plant, a time to reap,

a time to kill, a time to heal,

a time to tear down, a time to build up,

a time to weep, a time to laugh,

a time to mourn, a time to dance,

a time to embrace, a time to refrain from
embracing,

a time to find, a time to lose,

a time to keep, a time to throw away,

a time to tear, a time to mend,

a time to be silent, a time to speak,

a time to love, a time to hate,

a time for war, a time for peace.

VI. CREATIVITY/ IMAGINATION

31 "Imagination is the preview of coming attractions."

—Attributed to Albert Einstein

32 Creativity in Relationship

In the produce section of a large grocery store, the assistant manager noticed that one lady looked perplexed after she picked up a large grapefruit.

Walking over he asked if there was a problem, to which she replied, "This grapefruit is too large. I need only half a grapefruit but I can't find the price for half of one."

The young assistant manager smiled sagely and explained, "I'm sorry madam, but we don't sell grapefruits by the half (this was a while ago and, of course, stores do sell them now).

Well, the lady became irate and began objecting to this policy. To appease her, he told her he would check with his manager.

When the young man entered his manager's office, he explained to the manager that a lady complained to him about the store's policy of not selling grapefruits by the halves. What he didn't know was that the lady had followed him into the manager's office and heard him say his side of the story.

Suddenly, seeing the lady behind him, he thought for a second before adding, "And this nice lady has agreed to buy the other half."

After the now satisfied lady left, the impressed manager asked the young lad to sit down and congratulated him on how he handled this potentially explosive situation quite creatively. He asked where the young man was from. Proud that the manager had singled him out and anxious to respond with a bright response, he said, "I'm from Baltimore, sir, where they have a great football team but ugly women."

To which the manager's face dropped and the room temperature became much cooler. He indignantly replied, "Young man, my wife is from Baltimore." Berating himself for making such a major *faux pas*, he paused, gathered his wits, then meekly said, "What position did she play?"

There is a creative way to handle every situation.

33 "It is better to create than to learn! Creating is the essence of life."

—Julius Caesar (100 BC- 44 BC)
Roman General and Statesman

34 The Jill Bolte Taylor Story

Some people are aware that our brains are made up of two separate sides: the left is the logical side where we spend most of our time while the right side is the creative portion.

Like you, I, too, receive way too many wasteful e-mails every day. However, without a doubt, one of the most fascinating e-mails I've ever received was about a lady named Dr. Jill Bolte Taylor. Partly because she had a brother who suffered from the brain disorder of schizophrenia, she devoted her life to the study of the brain and primarily worked with stroke victims. In her own words, she admitted that she lived pretty much in the left side of her brain, the rational side, in trying to better understand the workings of the mind.

Ironically, this doctor who worked with stroke victims woke up one morning with a dull ache in her head that soon spread to nearly completely incapacitate her. Suddenly, she realized that she was in the middle of a stroke.

Even more ironic, this stroke shut down the left side of her brain, leaving her imprisoned in the right side. Do you know how she described this new imprisonment? She said, "It is so cool here. I feel like I'm in nirvana."

Being creative, utilizing your own creativity not only solves problems, but also just feels wonderful. Julius Caesar said that creativity is the essence of life.

35 "Imagination is more important than knowledge, because with imagination you can change reality."

—Attributed to Albert Einstein

36 The good news is that we do not have to have a stroke like Dr. Jill Bolte Taylor to shift to the creative, right side of the brain; there are many techniques available. The most common are prayer and meditation. However, my favorite is the one used by the greatest inventor of all time, Thomas Edison.

He would work on a problem, and work on a problem, and work on a problem. After lunch, he would sit in a chair with a large metal bowl on his lap. Holding two metal balls over the bowl, his arm resting on the armrest, he would take a nap.

As soon as he nodded off to sleep, his hand would relax, releasing the steel balls to fall into the metal bowl with a loud clang.

What is so fascinating, Edison said, is that when the metal balls dropped into the metal bowl, the loud clang would wake him up and "in that split second, I would sometimes receive the solution I had been seeking for months and months."

37 "Our Creator,
        Created Us,
        To Create."

—Maxwell Winston Stone

For more stories on creativity, go to www.ErnieCarwile.com and order the book, *The Magic of Creativity.*

VII. Commitment

38 "The act of committing to something invokes mystical powers; tenuous agreement suddenly becomes a solemn vow and extraordinary determination springs forth."

—Maxwell Winston Stone

39 The Coach's Story

I read a story that a football coach (I think it was the fabulous coach, Lou Holtz) told about the power of commitment. He recounted that, while in college and playing football, all his friends started getting married. He had been dating a woman for a while and thought that maybe marriage should just be the next step for him, too, so he asked this girl to marry him, which she did.

Well, after being married a short time, he started to have second thoughts that maybe he shouldn't have gotten married...maybe he really didn't even love his wife.

But, as he began having these thoughts,

suddenly football thoughts popped into his head and he reflected on why he was so successful in football. When it finally hit him, he knew the reason: because he was so committed to the game. Then, for whatever reason, his brain bridged the gap between football and his marriage and he began wondering, if his marriage was not working so well, maybe it was because he had not committed to it.

Right then, he committed himself to his young wife and shared that suddenly his wife became sweeter, more beautiful than ever before...and she seemed to even be a better cook.

40 "There are only two options regarding commitment: You're either IN or you're OUT. There is no such thing as life in-between."

—Pat Riley (1945-   )
Basketball Coach extraordinaire

41 The Famous Pig Story

A Pig and a Chicken were walking down the road. The Chicken said, "Yo Pig, I was thinking about us opening a restaurant."

"Yeah, and what would we call it?" the Pig asked.

"How about Ham N'Eggs?" the Chicken said.

After pondering on this for a bit, the Pig finally responded, "No thanks. I'd be committed while you'd only be involved."

Takes a minute, doesn't it. See, the Pig would have to give his life to provide the ham, while the Chicken only had to lay eggs.

42 "Make no doubt about it, commitment is the courage to say yes without any guarantees of success."

—Maxwell Winston Stone

VIII. DEATH—
WHERE DO WE GO
FROM HERE?

43 "Where life was so astonishing, why shouldn't death be anything less?"

44 The Water Bug Parable

In a small body of water lived a colony of water bugs; each generation lived like the other, always clinging to the muddy bottom, and forever gazing up through the murky waters at what seemed a source of light shining through. Every so often, one would accidently lose their grip on the bottom and float up into the light, never to be seen again.

While each generation forever pondered and debated the source of the light, as well as those who had drifted up into it, one advanced generation decided to do something about it. Calling all the water bugs together, the ruling body of elders decided they would draw straws; the one with the shortest would be the one to let go, float up toward the light, discover what it was then return to share his findings with all the others on the bottom.

The fateful drawing occurred. The shortest straw holder agreed to the frightening task, made a solemn vow to return, let go and immediately began the journey ascending up towards the light.

Up, up, up he floated, scared to death, yet all the while transfixed as the light grew brighter and brighter. After what seemed a very long while, the little bug finally reached the top only to discover he was in a small pond deep in the forest.

Here he saw that the bright light turned out to be a magnificent yellow sun. And before where everything had been filtered through the brown, murky water, now he beheld everything clearly in their rich, true colors. The lush green grasses and trees, the bright yellow and red flowers everywhere and the sky that held the mesmerizing, golden sunlight was the most beautiful blue color imaginable.

But, just as he was experiencing these wondrous sights, a sudden tiredness came over him, causing him to go into a deep, deep sleep.

Sometime later he awoke, still on the pond, though now he noticed he'd grown wings, had turned into a dragonfly and could actually fly through the blue sky, seeing even more beautiful sights. Flitting his wings, he soared and soared, never ceasing to be amazed, nor to appreciate his newfound freedom and paradise.

Suddenly he remembered his vow to return. Desperately, urgently, he had to return to the water bugs below to tell them of the paradise above. So with a drop of his wings, he flew straight down into the water at a fast speed. Splat! He hit the hard surface knocking himself out cold.

Later upon awakening, he tried again and again. Then twice more, each time knocking himself out longer. Finally, realizing he would be unable to return despite his promise, he now knew for certain each water bug below would have to find the truth for itself.

With that understanding, he flew off into the beautiful blue sky, with all the surrounding magnificent colors, basked in the bright yellow sunlight and lived happily for all eternity.

45 "Someone described death as simply home-sickness of the soul."

—Henry Wadsworth Longfellow (1807-1802)
American Poet

46 A Lesson on Death

One day, Max took me to Children's Hospital, a place I did not want to go but, with Max, you never have a chance to protest. As we entered the oncology ward, the kids squealed with delight because his visit brought story time.

Kids seemed to come from everywhere, ages ranging from six to twelve, some walked, some were in wheelchairs, some came with mobile I.V.'s. As Max began, I kept noticing out of the corner of my eye one little girl, head as bald as an egg, staring at me. I'm sure my body language and facial expression openly disclosed my discomfort at being there.

As soon as Max finished his first story and the clapping died down, the little girl walked over to me and whispered, "Hey mister, you don't have to be afraid. Everyone is going to die."

Her candor embarrassed me, but I was able to get out, "What's your name?"

"Angela," she said "What's yours?"

Then crawling up on my lap she said the most amazing thing. "I think I have it figured out," she said, "see, we're all given assignments here on earth—some of us are given longer assignments, and some of us are given shorter ones—mine's just shorter," she matter-of-factly said and smiled up at me with the most beautiful brown eyes. I thought how close the name Angela was to angel.

Out of the mouths of babes raced across my mind.

47 "What the caterpillar calls the end of the world, the Master calls a butterfly."

—Richard Bach (1936-   )
American Author

48 On Death

"I am standing on the seashore. A ship at my side spreads her white sails to the morning breeze and starts for the blue ocean.

I stand watching her until she fades on the horizon, that speck of white cloud just where the sea and the sky meet. Someone at my side says, "She is gone."

But gone where? The loss of sight is in me, not her.

And just at that moment when someone says, "She's gone," there are others on the other side watching her coming. "Here she comes," they shout with glee.

That is the way it is with dying."

—Henry Scott Holland (1847-1928)
Religious Professor of Divinity

49 Weary, he had traveled far, nearly spent. Was this finally it? Had he finally discovered the place which held that which he had sought for so long? So many other attempts...all futile... all dead ends. This lead had actually been a fluke. Had it been predestined by the gods?

Tying his tired horse to a tree, he began climbing the steep mountain. The thinner air caused him to frequently pause to catch his breath. Finally reaching the pinnacle, he saw only a small, cone-shaped stone hut, smoke rising from its chimney.

Knocking on the wind-faded door, he heard someone inside chuckle, then say, "Come in. I've been expecting you."

Perplexed, Sir Lancelot pushed open the thick, heavy-timbered door to see a tiny, wizened old man sitting in front a fire. "You have come long and far. Sit. Rest and I will give you what you have sought."

"The Holy Grail?" Sir Lancelot stuttered.

"Oh yes," the prophet answered, eyebrows arched, "but it is not a thing...it is the three most important questions a man can seek to answer: Where did we come from? Why am I here? Where will I go when I leave?

"But those are questions. I seek the cup from which our Lord Jesus drank at the Last Supper."

With an enigmatic smile, a bright gleam in his eye, he answered, "The true Holy Grail is not a possession one can hold, it is questions...the three most important questions any true seeker must ask himself."

For more stories on death, go to
www.ErnieCarwile.com and order the book,
Where Do We Go From Here:
Death, The Next Great Adventure.

IX. FORGIVENESS

50 "Always forgive your enemies. Nothing annoys them so much."

—Oscar Wilde (1854-1900)
Irish Author and Poet

51 The Lost Son

"I heard of quite a unique situation," Max said. "It was about a father who had gotten into a fight with his son and told him to leave home. His son's name was Juan and I think they were from South America.

"Well, after a couple of months of not hearing from the boy, one day the father broke down crying. Realizing his mistake, he frantically searched all over, everywhere, but no luck. As a last resort he had an idea. He would place an advertisement in the city's largest newspaper, a large ad that anyone reading the newspaper could not miss. The ad went something like this: 'Juan, my beloved son, forgive me. I love and miss you so. Please come back home. I'll meet you at 12:00 noon this Saturday at the city's town square by the statue. Your loving father.'

"Saturday morning arrived; the father got up early, eagerly awaiting the time to leave. However, as he approached the town square, he came upon a large crowd of young men, all gathered around the statue, all diligently looking around. Unable to make his way, he asked a young man standing on the outside what all the commotion was about. Excitedly, the young man said his name was Juan, and he was responding to an ad his father had placed asking him to come home!"

Finishing, Max said, "That South American father never found his son, though he stayed and searched all afternoon."

52 "And throughout all eternity; I forgive you, you forgive me."

—William Blake (1757-1827)
English Poet

53 The Prayer of St. Francis

Lord, make me an instrument of thy peace.

Where there is hatred, let me sow love;

Where there is injury, pardon;

Where there is doubt, faith;

Where there is despair, hope;

Where there is darkness, light;

Where there is sadness, joy.

O divine Master, grant that

I may not so much seek...

To be consoled as to console;

To be understood as to understand;

To be loved as to love;

For it is in giving that we receive;

It is in pardoning that we are pardoned;

It is in dying to self that we are born to
eternal self.

54 Daily Prayer: "I forgive everybody, everything, every day."

55 It has been said that when Leonardo da Vinci was painting "The Last Supper," he painted the pictures of the twelve disciples' faces, their facial features, from his memory of people he actually knew that reminded him of each disciple.

And, when it came time to paint the face of Judas he unthinkingly began painting the face of his most despised enemy. Completing this he went on to paint the last facial picture of Jesus. But as hard as he tried, he couldn't do it as he kept looking nervously over at the face of Judas. He would think he was just about finished with Jesus' face, when his eyes would again and again return to Judas' face, and he could never finish painting Jesus' face.

Frustrated, he wondered why this was occurring until it finally dawned on him; he could not paint Jesus' face until he had forgiven his most hated enemy. So he did just that, and when he returned to the painting, this time he easily finished the face of Jesus.

X. HUMOR

56 "Humor is mankind's greatest blessing."

—Mark Twain (1835-1910)
American Humorist

57 Here are some good one-liners to use:

➢ How do you tell when you are out of invisible ink?

➢ Borrow money from pessimists—they don't expect it back.

➢ When everything is coming your way, you're in the wrong lane.

➢ Half the people you know are below average.

➢ What happens when you get scared half to death twice?

➢ 99% of the lawyers give the rest a bad name.

➢ All those who believe in psychokinesis raise my hand.

➢ If at first you don't succeed, skydiving is not for you.

➢ Why do psychics have to ask you for your name?

➢ Everyone has a photographic memory; some just don't have film.

➢ If your car could travel at the speed of light, would your headlights work?

➢ A clear conscience is usually a sign of a bad memory.

58 "When speaking to an audience, humor is what makes them want to have you back."

—Maxwell Winston Stone

59 A wealthy farmer decided to go to church on Christmas Eve. After the services, he approached the minister with great enthusiasm. "Reverend," he exclaimed, "the sermon you gave was damned good!"

"Why thank you," the minister responded, "but your compliment would have been much better if you hadn't cursed."

"My apologies," said the farmer, "but it was so damned good that I put a $100 bill in the collection basket."

"The hell you say," the surprised minister retorted without thinking.

60 "Outside of a dog, a book is man's best friend; inside of a dog, it's too dark to read."

—Groucho Marx (1890-1977)
American Comedian

61 "If there are no dogs in Heaven, then when I die I want to go where they went."

—Will Rogers (1879-1933)
American Humorist

62 "The reason a dog has so many friends is that he wags his tail rather than his tongue."

63 "If I were more like my dog, I'd be a better human being."

—Ernie Carwile (1947-   )

Author

For more quotes and stories on dogs and other animals, go to www.ErnieCarwile.com and order, *And The Animals Shall Teach Us: Angels In Disguise.*

XI. THE POWER OF LISTENING

64 "Before you speak, it is necessary for you to listen, for God speaks in the silence of the heart."

—Mother Theresa (1920-1997)
Catholic Sister and Missionary

65 I heard that a communications professor once made a huge and most surprising discovery. He offered two courses in communication: one entitled, "Effective Communication;" the other, "Effective Listening." Both courses listed the exact same curriculum; but what was startling was that the course on "Effective Communication" filled up so quickly they had to offer another one...while the other course on "Effective Listening" was dropped because not a single student signed up!

66 "Most successful people I know are the ones who do more listening than speaking."

—Bernard Baruch (1870-1965)
American Financier

67 Just Listen

I need you to just listen to me.

Please don't give me advice; that's not what I asked. Advice is cheap. $1 will get me "Dear Abby."

Nor do I need you to tell me that I shouldn't feel a certain way when that is exactly the way I feel.

And, please don't try to solve my problem; that is for me to do.

Just hear me out. That's all I'm asking you to do—just listen. You don't have to talk or do anything else.

I'm not hopeless or helpless; just confused.

When you try to do things for me that I need to do for myself, then you are contributing to my weaknesses.

The truth is that I do feel the way I do even if it seems irrational to you. Please simply accept the way that I feel without trying to correct me; then I can quit trying to convince you and try to understand why I am feeling so irrational. See, I actually believe that, when I understand this, the answers I need will become obvious.

68 "You cannot truly listen to anyone and do anything else at the same time."

—M. Scott Peck (1936-2005)
Psychiatrist and Bestselling Author

69 Little Girl Playing

A little girl was outside playing by herself in the backyard, and every once in a while, she would stop what she was doing and be very still.

Her mother was observing her from the kitchen window, saw her doing this odd action and suddenly remembered she had seen her doing this before. When the little girl came in her mother asked why she would suddenly stop playing and be very still.

The little girl nonchalantly responded, "Oh, I'm just stopping and listening to see if God has anything to tell me."

70 "One of the best ways to persuade others is with your ears—by listening to them."

—Dean Rusk (1909-1994)
Longest Serving Secretary of State
in the U. S. History

71 I have learned a great, great secret.

I start off each day with a period of listening. By that, I mean that, during my prayer/meditation time, I plan a portion of it to just listen to what the Universe has to say to me.

Sometimes, what I hear may be practical things, things that will benefit my everyday life; sometimes I hear things to use in my books; other times I might be given insights into the workings of the world.

It is wonderful. It's like having my own information angel enlightening me on the road to life. And it all came about by not talking or plea bargaining—or wishing—but by simply listening.

Obviously an art form rarely used anymore, I wonder if listening may be the key to transforming our individual lives and the world.

—Ernie Carwile

XII. Oh, The Oneness of Us All

72 "Human beings have a kind of optical illusion. We see ourselves as separate, rather than a part of the whole."

Albert Einstein (1879-1955)
German-born Theoretical Physicist

73 The fable of the Hundredth Monkey Phenomenon:

In 1952 on the island of Koshima, Japan, monkeys called Macaca fuscata were observed over a thirty-year period. Scientists had been providing the monkeys with sweet potatoes which the monkeys loved, except for when sand got on them.

One day a young female monkey accidently dropped the sand-dirtied potato into the ocean thereby washing off the irritating sand. She eventually showed her sand washing technique to her family and playmates, who in turn taught it to their family and friends and this idea passed slowly throughout the island.

What seemed an insignificant discovery observed by the scientists between the years 1952 and 1958 suddenly became something miraculous in the fall of 1958. At some point when perhpaps the one-hundredth monkey on the island learned this new technique, every monkey knew to wash the sweet potatoes to remove the sand by that evening!

Furthermore, these scientists next observed that the practice of washing the sweet potatoes spontaneously jumped over to another island that was completely unattached to the first island!

From a scientific point of view, there was no logical explanation for this to happen. From a metaphysical viewpoint, a theory emerged: at a point when a certain number of people grasp a new idea, say "one hundred," then the idea somehow spreads or communicates to all the people on our planet.

74 "Did you know that humans are genetically 99.95% identical? How then can we fight, kill and be prejudiced with one another when we are very nearly identical?"

—Ernie Carwile

75 Often-times churches in America are too homogeneous, meaning that each church attracts pretty much the same kind of people.

To counteract this tendency, in one of my churches, I had a sign built and placed at the entrance into the church. It simply said:

We Reserve the Right to Accept Everyone!

76 "To believe your own thought, to believe that what is true for you in your private heart is true for all men—that is genius."

—Ralph Waldo Emerson (1803-1882)
American Author

77 Oh, The Oneness of Us All

As the world is a circle, and we are all
contained within,

How could it be otherwise, that we are not
one within?

Fight and strife, we battle so hard, for it is
us who cause the pain.

Yet how could we harm that part of us,
that's also part of the same?

In truth, we are closer than close, hearts
sharing the same space.

It's absurd to think I can harm you,
without harming myself.

I am you and you are me,
though uniqueness still exists.

And this truth of oneness,
can never, ever desist.

Oh, the oneness of us all...

—Ernie Carwile

78 You can easily break a single stick. But tie a bunch together into a bundle, and you can't break them. It's the same for us; together we are stronger.

79 "I believe we are all angels with only one wing, and we can only fly by embracing one another."

—Luciano de Crescenzo (1928-   )
Italian Writer and Director

For more stories and quotes on oneness, go to www.ErnieCarwile.com and order the book, *Oh, The Oneness of Us All.*

XIII. PERSISTENCE: THE ART OF FAILING UNTIL YOU SUCCEED

80 "Failure is the path of least persistence."

—Maxwell Winston Stone

81 The Bamboo Tree

There is a most unusual tree that grows in China. Its uniqueness is that, after planting it, the farmer will weed, fertilize and water it for a full year, but nothing happens.

The same thing is done for the second year. He weeds, fertilizes, and waters it, but still nothing can be seen.

What is so interesting is that this continues for the third year and the fourth year. Each year the farmer has been vigilant in weeding, fertilizing and watering.

But, in the fifth year something absolutely amazing happens; the tree suddenly breaks through the ground and miraculously grows sixty feet in only six weeks!

How? Because of the farmer's persistence.

Though he could see no results, the tree had been growing the most intricate root system, all the while hidden from above.

82 "You are always free to change your mind and do something different. But at some point, to achieve success, you must decide to take a stand and not let anyone convince you otherwise."

—Maxwell Winston Stone

83 There was a high school student who finally became serious about his grades his senior year. He studied hard and made straight A's that final year. The problem, he soon discovered, was that he had goofed off his first three years and gotten lousy grades. Even though he had received all A's his last year, his earlier poor grades kept his grade-point low.

But still determined to go to college, he selected his top five choices, carefully filled out each school's application, and, along with his high school transcripts, optimistically mailed them off to each college's admissions department.

It took four weeks for him to receive his first rejection, five weeks to receive the next two, and six weeks to receive the fourth rejection. Still hopeful, after eight weeks, he received his fifth and final one, and something inside him snapped.

Now, rather than feel sorry for himself, he sat down and composed a new letter to the last college that rejected him. The letter said, "Dear Admissions Officer, I am in receipt of your rejection of my application, along with the four other rejections I received from other colleges. As much as I know I should just accept your decline, I find I cannot and therefore I must reject your rejection. I am informing you, I will appear for classes on September 15th."

Well, you can imagine how the admissions secretary responded to his letter. Her first response was to haughtily throw it into the trash—which she did. But, the young man's letter kept bugging her until she finally realized that anyone who wanted into her college that badly just might end up being quite an asset.

She explained to the admissions committee her reasoning and they unanimously reversed the earlier decision.

Five years later that young man graduated with honors.

84 "The more I practice, the luckier I get."

—Gary Player (1935-
Professional Golfer

85 "Nothing in the world can take the place of persistence.

"Talent will not; nothing is more common than talented, unsuccessful men. Genius will not; unrewarded genius is almost a proverb. Education will not; the world is full of educated derelicts.

"Persistence and determination alone...has solved and always will solve the problems of the human race."

—Calvin Coolidge (1872-1933)
Thirtieth President of the U. S.

86 There is a book that was published forty or so years ago and I've been unable to find another copy; but this is one of those books that every human being should be required to read. Written by John White, it's entitled *Rejection*, and just listen to what White says.

"Rejection," White writes, "is a much abused word, one we often think means failure, though that isn't so." He cited the following: "Twentieth Century Fox rejected the movie *Jaws* outright, for they believed it would be a box office failure; Universal Studios, believing that science fiction movies don't sell really well, rejected *Star Wars*; Decca Recording Company, one of the largest in the industry at that time, in 1962 said this about the Beatles: 'We don't like their sound. Besides, groups with guitars are on their way out. This group will never make it.'"

White also listed books and authors (near and dear to my heart) that have had their works rejected: *The Tale of Peter Rabbit* was rejected by six publishing houses before the author, Beatrix Potter, cashed in her life savings to publish it herself; *Peyton Place* was rejected by fourteen publishers; *Jonathan Livingston Seagull* was rejected by twenty publishers. The poet e.e. cummings couldn't get a publisher; his mother scraped together all she could so they could self-publish and sold millions of poems.

"What is really neat is what he wrote on the dedication page of his first book: 'No thanks to...' and then he listed all of the publishers who turned him down."

White's magnificent point, and one all of us should never, ever forget, is to provide us with the courage and persistence to continue believing in our work even when our ideas are rejected.

87 "If at first you don't succeed, try, try again. Then quit. No use being a damn fool about it."

—W. C. Fields (1880-1946)
Comedian

For more stories and quotes on persistence, go to www.ErnieCarwile.com and order the book, *Persistence: The Art Of Failing Until You Succeed.*

XIV. LIVING IN THE PRESENT

88 "To see the world in a grain of sand; and a heaven in a wild flower; hold infinity in the palm of your hand; and eternity in an hour."

—William Barclay (1907-1978)
Scottish Author and Theologian

89 The Dream

I had a dream in which I was guaranteed that my bank account would be credited with $86,400 every single day. I was told I could spend this money on anything I wanted, anything that made my life easier for me, anything that would bring me more wholesome enjoyment and a deepening appreciation of life.

There was just one stipulation: at the end of every twenty-four hour period, all remaining unspent cash would be lost; wiped off the account; meaning no money could be accumulated. However, what proved interesting was that a new $86,400 would be credited back to the account every new day.

Now, this was one of those dreams that really stuck with you; like one of those itsy-bitsy nearly invisible stickers in one of your fingers that slightly though persistently irritates you throughout the day until you finally get home to get some tweezers. It wasn't until the next morning as I was doing my morning crossword puzzle along with coffee when my inner psyche disclosed the meaning.

The crossword puzzle asked what XX times III was. Remembering my Roman numerals, on the newspaper I multiplied twenty times three and got sixty. Then, my mind suddenly bridged some gap and for no explainable reason and I recalled that there were sixty seconds in a minute, then sixty minutes in an hour and finally twenty-four hours each day. So I multiplied sixty times sixty times twenty-four and scribbled in the margin the number 86,400...and gasped.

My mind whirling, I suddenly understood my dream. The money was only symbolic of time and the dream was challenging me see how I was using my time every day: Was I wasting it or using it well?

90 *Carpe diem* is one of the most famous quotes of any time. It means to seize the day, to live in the immediate present, because you have no assurance of what will happen in the future.

91 Do you remember Sen. Paul Tsongas?

At the age of only forty-three, he stunned Washington a while back when he suddenly announced he would not run again for Congress. Suffering from only a mild case of cancer that the doctors assured him had a very high probability of a cure, which would likely would allow him to complete a second term, Tsongas explained he had decided to quit politics after spending a weekend at home with his wife and three daughters, ages three to ten.

"One night my children went to sleep with my arms around them," Tsongas recalled, "and I realized for the next seven years this might rarely happen. Now I walk my kids to school and think about them, not politics, and my life is much richer."

He added, "Someone once gave me some very good advice: No one on their deathbed ever said they wished they had spent more time at work!"

92 "If there is a sin against life, it consists perhaps not so much in disparaging of life as in hoping for another life and in eluding the implacable grandeur of this life."

—Albert Camus (1913-1960)
French Nobel Prize Winner

93 I read this story in one of Leo Buscaglia's books, *Living, Loving and Learning.* It makes a rather subtle yet powerful point on the importance of all of us remembering to say and do what we need to say to our loved ones now, when we have the opportunity to do so, rather than wait and do it at some time in the future, which may never come. Buscaglia said it had been given to him by a young girl who wished to remain anonymous. This is what she wrote about her fiancé:

"Remember the day I borrowed your brand new car and dented it? I thought you'd kill me, but you didn't... And remember the time I dragged you to the beach, and you said it was going rain, and it did? I thought you'd say 'I told you so.' But you didn't...Do you remember the time I flirted with all the guys to make you jealous, and you were?...I thought you'd leave me then, but you didn't...Do you remember the time I spilled strawberry pie all over your car rug? I'd thought you'd hit me, but you didn't...And remember the time I forgot to tell you the dance was formal, and you showed up in jeans? I thought you'd drop me, but you didn't."

And then the young woman wrote, "There were lots of things you didn't do. But you put up with me, and you loved me, and you protected me. And there were lots of things I wanted to make up to you when you returned from Viet Nam...but you didn't."

XV. THE INSIDIOUSNESS OF *PREJUDICE*

94 "Men hate each other because they fear each other; they fear each other because they don't know each other; they don't know each other because they are separated from each other."

—Martin Luther King (1929-1968)
American Civil Rights Leader

95 "In Germany, the Nazi's first came for the Socialists, and I didn't speak up because I wasn't a Socialist.

Then they came for the Communists, and I didn't speak up because I wasn't a Communist.

Next they came for the Trade Unionists but I didn't speak up because I wasn't a Trade Unionist.

Then they came for the Jews, and I didn't speak up because I wasn't a Jew.

Finally, they came for me, and there was no one left to speak up for me."

—Martin Niemoller (1892-1984)
German Anti-Nazi Theologian

96 "No man is an island entire of itself; every man is a piece of the Continent, a part of the main...any man's death diminishes me, because I am involved in Mankind; And therefore never send to know for whom the bell tolls; it tolls for thee."

—John Donne (1572-1631)
English Poet and Writer of Prose

97 A while back the book, *Black Like Me,* written by a white author named John Howard Griffith, focused on the prejudice, pain and separation black-skinned people in the U. S. experienced.

Coming from a middle-income white family, the author admitted that he'd had little first-hand interaction with blacks. So to learn, he did some rather radical things to change his external appearance: took pills to darken his skin pigment, dyed himself all over, shaved his head, wore brown-colored contact lenses, worked on a dialect and began living among black persons.

Do you know what he discovered?

It is something no one should ever forget. He discovered, the hard way, that when you get to know the unknown person—that is, any person seemingly different—you will find we are all the same.

98 "Prejudice, the dislike of all that is unlike."

—Israel Zangwill (1864-1926)
British Humorist and Writer

XVI. THE GREATEST CHALLENGE OF ALL— *SELF-ACCEPTANCE*

99 "To thine own self be true, and it must follow, as the night the day, thou canst then be false to any man."

—William Shakespeare (1564-1616)
The Greatest Writer in the English Language

100 I first read this poem in one of Ann Landers' columns. Called, "The Man In the Glass," it was mailed to her by a young woman whose brother was trying to get off drugs. They thought he was doing better when he suddenly killed himself. This poem was found taped to his bathroom mirror:

"When you get what you want in your struggle for self, and the world makes you king for a day, just go to a mirror and look at yourself, and see what that man has to say. For it isn't your father or mother or wife, whose judgment upon you must pass, the fellow whose verdict counts most in your life, is the one staring back from the glass. Some people might think you you're a straight-shootin' chum and call you a wonderful guy, but the man in the glass says you're only a bum, if you can't look him straight in the eye. He's the fellow to please, never mind the rest, for he's with you clear up to the end. And you've passed your most dangerous, difficult task if the guy in the glass is your friend. You may fool the whole world down the pathways of years, and get pats on your back as you pass. But the final reward will be heartaches and tears if you've cheated the man in the glass."

101 Every person born into this world represents something new, something that never existed before, something original and unique.

It is the duty of every person to know: there never has been anyone like him [her] in this world, for if there had been someone like them, there would have been no need for that person to be in the world.

Every single person is a new thing in the world and is called upon to fulfill their particularity in this world.

—Martin Buber (1878-1965)
Austrian-born Jewish Philosopher

102 "To be nobody—but yourself—in a world that is doing its best, night and day, to make you into everybody else—means to fight the hardest battle which any human can fight."

—e. e. cummings (1894-1962)
American Poet

103 Old Hindu Legend

There was a time when all men and women were gods, but so abused their divinity and power that Brahma, the chief god, decided to take away their divine power; where to hide it became the chief concern.

Calling all the ruling gods into council to solve the dilemma, their first solution was, "We will hide man and woman's divinity on the tallest of tall mountain peaks in the entire world." But Brahma, after considering their proposed solution concluded that that would not work, for eventually someone would scale the highest mountaintop and find it.

After further thought, the group then proposed, "We'll hide their divinity in the deepest spot in all the oceans." But again Brahma said no, for humans would soon develop the means to descend to the deepest depths.

Finally, after much debate, the ruling gods concluded, "We don't know where to hide their divinity because there is no place on all the earth or in the sea that men and women will eventually discover."

After much thought, Brahma finally proclaimed, "I know a place where they will never think to look...We'll hide it within themselves."

And ever since, the legend concludes, men

and women have been going up and down the earth, searching for that something called divinity. Of course never taking the time, never seeking the silence, in the one place they never looked—inside themselves!

104 "If a man [or woman] does not keep pace with his companions, perhaps it is because he hears a different drum. Let him step to the music he hears, however measured or far away."

—Henry David Thoreau (1817-1862)
American Author, Philosopher, Novelist

105 "And what is that part of you that causes the greatest shame? What causes you the greatest guilt?" the keeper at the gates of Heaven asked.

"I could never share that," the soldier whispered, "it is too horrible...I was too horrible."

Staring into the soldier's eyes for what seemed an eternity, the Keeper implored. "But that is the part of you that is missing; that is the part you must accept and bring with you for you to enter into the Kingdom of Heaven."

"Are you nuts?" the soldier screamed. "If you knew what I did you would never let me in."

"Oh no," the Gatekeeper assured, "that is the part that is now most needed...for it completes you, allows you to be whole and allows you to enter."

Falling on his knees, the soldier confessed his atrocities and the gate gently swung open.

106 "God created you unique. Never change simply because you're outnumbered!"

—Max

For more stories and quotes on self-acceptance, go to www.ErnieCarwile.com and order the book, *Never Good Enough*.

XVII. SERVICE

107 "The fragrance always remains on the hand that gives the rose."

—Mahatma Gandhi (1869-1948)
Leader of Nonviolent Civil Disobedience

108 True Story

The late author Leo Buscaglia said that he was once asked to judge a contest to find the most caring person.

Believe it or not, the winner turned out to be a four-year-old boy. The young boy's elderly neighbor had just lost his wife. One day, seeing the old man crying out in his backyard, the little boy walked over, climbed in the old gentleman's lap and just sat there.

When the little boy returned home, his mother, who had watched him sitting on the old man's lap, asked him what he had said.

The little boy just said, "Nothing, I just sat on his lap and helped him cry."

You see, all of us can provide a service of some kind.

⁕

109 "The sole meaning of life is to serve humanity."

—Leo Tolstoy (1828-1910)
Russian Author

⁕

110 The Dead Sea

Throughout my life, I have been fortunate to have connected numerous times with the importance of doing "service."

Of course, the difference between hearing something versus actually incorporating it into your daily life is huge. It has been said before that the greatest distance is the one it takes to move something from your head to your heart.

This truth about the necessity of giving

service was reinforced to me one day while waiting in a dentist office and reading a *National Geographic* magazine covering the Dead Sea. The article gave an excellent explanation about how this body of water was created and I suddenly understood that the reason it is called the Dead Sea is because it only receives water and does not give any back. For whatever reason, this time when I heard this factual piece of data, I suddenly bridged the understanding that we humans are the same—if we only receive in our lives and never give back anything, we, too, will dry up spiritually and die.

Furthermore, this idea was followed with remembering that the act of breathing is a two-part action first involving inhaling, or receiving oxygen; the second, exhaling, or giving back carbon dioxide. Living on planet earth, this is quite a phenomenal give-take situation. We breathe in the oxygen needed to survive that the plants give off and exhale carbon dioxide, a gas plants need to exist. This is called a symbiotic relationship and,

CRÈME de la CRÈME

what is of dire importance to remember, is both parts are intimately interrelated: giving and receiving. That is the point of this book: if both parts do not occur, it is crystal clear that humans, vegetation and our planet will surely die.

Perhaps, for the first time, I came to fully comprehend the importance of giving and receiving; that it is not just a cute little adage, but a vitally important aspect of living.

111 I can still recall the surprise I felt after reading, for the first time, a quote by the famed medical doctor, musician, theologian and missionary Dr. Albert Schweitzer. Speaking to a class of business-school graduates, he made the statement: "I don't know what your destinies will be, but the one thing I do know is that the only ones among you who will be really happy are those who will have sought and found how to serve."

112 "I shall pass through this world but once; any good thing, therefore, that I can do, or any kindness that I can show to any human being or animal, let me do it now, let me not defer it or neglect, for I shall not pass this way again."

—John Galsworthy ((1867-1933)
English Novelist and Playwright

113 Giving Only To Receive

There is a fable which beautifully depicts this truth:

One day while out walking, a very poor but proud Scotsman heard someone yelling for help. Quickly walking towards the panicked voice, he came upon a bog where a young boy had become mired up to his waist and was slowly sinking. With little thought as to his own safety he waded in and was able to rescue the lad.

The next day, a beautiful carriage arrived at the Scotsman's humble little hut and an elegantly dressed man got out, thanked him for saving his son and offered him a large reward. The proud Scotsman refused the reward but accepted the man's thanks.

When the rich man saw the farmer's son watching the scenario, he changed his tactic and instead offered, "Let me take your son and give him a good education. If the lad is anything like his father, he'll grow into a man to be proud of."

The Scotsman, knowing his son would never have an opportunity like this, finally agreed and the two men shook hands in agreement.

Many years later, the Scotsman's son graduated from the Saint Mary's Hospital Medical School in London and later was knighted Sir Alexander Fleming for his discovery of penicillin.

Years after this, a most ironic event took place; the nobleman's son contracted pneumonia and was saved only because penicillin had been discovered by the Scotsman's son, now known as Sir Alexander Fleming.

Even more ironic was that the nobleman's name was Lord Randolph Churchill and his son was none other than Sir Winston Churchill!

114 "Service is the rent you pay for having a place here on earth."

—Mohammed Ali (1942-)
Former Heavyweight
Champion of the world

XVIII. SUCCESS/FAILURE

115 "I'm finding that success is harder to deal with than failure...in fact, failure teaches us much more than success."

—Shirley MacLaine (1934-)
Actress and Author of *Out on a Limb*

116 A rich, high-powered New York investment banker finally got away for a much needed vacation to a quiet, small coastal Mexican village. Relaxing, staring out at the mesmerizing sea late one morning, he happened to witness a lone fisherman returning from what was, obviously, a most successful fishing outing. As the Mexican man unloaded two rather large yellow-fin tuna, the American asked the fisherman, who seemed to be about his age, how long it took to catch the fish.

"Not very long," the fisherman explained. "See, I know where the fish are."

The American then asked the fisherman why he didn't stay out longer and catch more.

The fisherman modestly explained, "I only catch enough for my family to eat."

The banker pressed further, "But, what do you do the rest of your day?"

"Oh, I sleep later in the mornings before I go fishing," he said. Then after fishing for a little while, I return home and play with my children, eat a fresh baked roll my wife usually makes and drink a cup of my favorite coffee. By then it's usually time to take a siesta with my wife." Continuing, he added, "Then I walk over to the plaza where I drink cervezas with my amigos and play a little guitar...or sometimes we might play dominoes until after dark." Smiling, the fisherman nodded his head, "I have quite a wonderful and full life."

The astonished banker couldn't believe his ears. His mind quickly cranked up, going a mile a minute, and he said, "Listen, I could help you. I could make you rich."

Perplexed, the fisherman asked, "But how?"

Mind whirling, the American blurted out, "I have an MBA from Harvard, so listen closely. If you got up much earlier in the mornings, spent more time out on the sea and caught more fish, you would soon have more money to buy a whole fleet of fishing boats."

The Mexican fisherman politely stood listening to the wound-up American.

"Eventually, you could build a fish-processing plant and then sell out to a big corporation and make a ton of money."

Eyes twinkling, the fisherman replied, "Ah, so you mean I could then move to a small quiet village on the coast, sleep late in the mornings, fish a little, play with my children, take a siesta with my wife and, in the evenings, walk to the plaza where I could sip cervezas with my amigos while we play our guitars and sing."

117 "Never let the fear of striking out keep you from going up to the plate."

—Babe Ruth (1895-1948)
American Baseball Player

118 A young graduate from a seminary was assigned to his first church and seemed to fail miserably at most ministerial tasks, especially with sermons. Never having done any public speaking before, he sensed that all he needed was some time to develop this skill.

His bishop heard about his dull sermons and visited the congregation. In the middle of the service, when the young minister was struggling with the sermon, the bishop stood up and harshly criticized the young man's novice attempts.

Everyone expected the young minister would quit after being so publicly humiliated.

Surprised that the minister was present at the next Sunday service and still determined to succeed, the young minister walked to the pulpit and very quietly spoke these words:

"I can sin. You can sin. And the bishop can sin.

"I can make mistakes. You can make mistakes. The bishop can make mistakes.

"I could go to hell. You could go to hell. And the bishop can go to hell!"

Then he told the congregation he would see them next Sunday and try to present a better sermon.

119 "The greatest mistake you can make in life is to continually fear that you will make one."

—Elbert Hubbard (1856-1915)
American Writer and Philosopher

120 Was He Successful?

In 1831 he failed in business,

In 1832 he was defeated for the legislature,

In 1833 he again failed in business,

In 1835 his sweetheart died,

In 1836 he had a nervous breakdown,

In 1843 he was defeated in Congress,

In 1855 he was defeated for the Senate,

In 1856 he lost the race for the vice-presidency,

In 1858 he was again defeated for the Senate.

In 1860 he was elected President of the United States.

XIX. THE POWER OF SILENCE

121 "Silence allows you to find yourself; when that happens, the possibilities are endless."

—Maxwell Winston Stone

122 From all of Max's stories, this is one of my favorites.

There is a tribe in South America who decided they needed to move to find better water and hunting. After sending scouts to find the best place and listening to what they discovered, they made their decision.

During their journey, a spiritual leader of the tribe was assigned to determine when they should stop and rest and when it was time to go. Sometimes stops would last for only a day; other times they might camp for three or four days. One man who was very keen on them arriving at their final destination angrily questioned the spiritual leader, "Why do we stop so often and why do we sometimes stay so long?"

The spiritual leader's response bears remembering: "Because we have to wait for our spirits to catch up with us."

123 "Being constantly subjected to outside stimuli prevents us from responding to inside stimuli."

—Maxwell Winston Stone

124 Like the settling that occurs after you drop a large rock into a pond, at first the water is agitated, frothing; particles on the bottom are loosened up to make it impossible to see the bottom; whatever is lying beneath the surface is now hidden—just like the mind is when filled with noise.

Only stillness can calm the water. Only stillness can make it clear again so you can see all the way to the bottom.

What truths lie hidden from you because your mind is so busy, so stirred up, so agitated?

It is the silence that will calm your mind and allow you to once again to see clearly all the way to the deepest recesses of your soul. It allows us to separate the important from the extraneous, the wheat from the chaff. Silence allows us to rediscover the rhythm of life we so crave.

125 "Silence removes the veil between us and God."

—Max

126 Max's face was scrunched up. I'd been secretly watching him for a while; aware that his new expression indicated he had finally come to some unique understanding.

Sure enough, he began after clearing his throat to get my full attention.

"There is one particular passage in the New Testament, Ernie, that has forever baffled me. I think it's in the book of John, but it's about the adulterous woman. See, the Pharisees and Scribes were trying to trick Jesus by bringing him this woman who, according to Jewish law, was to be stoned, and asked him what he thought should be done.

"Now, this is the part that has always confused me for it said that, after being asked that highly loaded question, Jesus bent down and began writing with his finger in the sand.

"I mean, just think about the setting here—a woman's life was hanging by a thread and the tension must have been great. But Jesus' response was to drop down and begin writing in the sand. Why?"

I, too, had been bewildered over this action and had wondered myself why in the world Jesus did it.

Max responded, "It took me a long time

to figure this out. At least for me, I believe that when Jesus dropped down and wrote on the ground, this act allowed him to go within himself—kind of like doodling frees up your mind—and he listened and heard from God the exact combination of words, perhaps the only combination, which would defuse the whole situation. He then said the famous passage, 'Let him who is without sin among you cast the first stone.'

"Ernie, Jesus talked a lot about going into your closet and speaking directly with God, but I always thought it to be figurative," Max gazed intently at me.

"But now I see he meant it to be literal—that you and I can also go inside ourselves and tap into God's unlimited wisdom."

As my mind reeled, a question in my mind crystallized: could we all use this same resource, God, as easily as did Jesus?

127 "It is better to keep your mouth closed and let people think you are a fool than to open it and remove all doubt."

—Mark Twain (1835-1910)
American Humorist and Author

For more stories and quotes on The Power of Silence, go to www.ErnieCarwile.com and order the book, *The Power of Silence.*

XX. On Having a Sense of Values

128 "A half lie is still a lie."

—Benjamin Franklin (1706-1790)
Author, Printer and Statesman

129 This story was attributed to Ronald Reagan when he was Governor of California, although I've never been able to substantiate it.

Gov. Reagan told a story about an incident that happened when Bud Wilkinson had so many great national football teams in Oklahoma. Well, towards the end of the close of one season, he took his winning football team to a very mediocre Texas Christian team. On that day, T.C.U. played better than it had ever played before and, in the closing seconds, a receiver from T.C.U. dove into the end zone and made a spectacular catch for what seemed the winning touchdown.

A huge upset was in view. The crowd was going wild, when way down in the end zone, the player who had supposedly caught the ball, walked over to the referee and said, "Sir, the ball touched the ground before I caught it. It's not a touchdown."

Now, what would your reaction be? Do you think that maybe the kid had gone too far—been too honest? You know the referee hadn't seen it, so maybe he should have just shut his mouth?—OR SHOULD HE?

Governor Reagan then said, "Someday that young man may represent us in the Statehouse, in Congress, or even in the White House. And what then? Do we want him to keep his mouth shut if no one is looking?... Do you want him to make decisions that are based on political expediency...Or do you want him to make his decisions based upon the same kind of inner moral conviction that made him tell the truth to the referee without being asked?

And then Gov. Reagan closed the story by asking us all, "Who will teach them that kind of morality if it isn't you and me?"

130 "Honesty is the first chapter in the book of Wisdom."

—Thomas Jefferson (1743-1826)
Third U.S. President

131 The first time I read Edwin Arlington Robinson's poem, "Richard Corey," I was a junior high school, and though I didn't fully understand its meaning, it still haunted me. Listen to the poem and see how it affects your understanding about the value and meaning of life:

"Whenever Richard Cory went downtown,

we people on the pavement looked at him:

he was a gentleman from sole to crown,

clean favored, and imperially slim.

And he was always quietly arrayed,

and he was always human when he talked;

but still he fluttered pulses when he said,

"Good morning," and he glittered when he
    walked.

And he was rich—yes richer than a king—
and admirably schooled in every grace:
in fine, we thought that he was everything
to make us wish that we were in his place.

So we worked and waited for the light,
and went without meat, and cursed the
    bread;
and Richard Cory, one calm summer night,
went home and put a bullet through his
    head!"

132 "Wise persons have discovered that the
key to happiness is not having more, but
needing less."

—Maxwell Winston Stone

133 Bonus—There was a very rich man who wished for his young son to appreciate their wealth and rich city living by experiencing what it was like to be poor.

So he drove around in the country looking for a farm that was rather shabby, stopped to meet the family and spent time with them to insure they were good people, and made a financial deal for his son to spend the summer with the family.

Two months later he picked up his son and was most eager to hear what his son had learned. Driving home he asked the boy what he had discovered about the difference between being rich and poor. Thinking deeply, the boy finally spoke. "Well," he said, "I saw that where we only have one pet because we live in a condominium, they have four dogs and two cats—where we have a small swimming pool, they have a huge pond where we swam every day—where we buy all of our vegetables in a grocery store, they grow their own and they taste much better—where we have a couple of security guards to protect us, they have a lot of neighbors who watch out for each other—where we don't really own any land, they own forty acres."

The stunned father didn't know what to say. His son concluded his observations with the statement, "Thanks, Dad, for showing me how poor we are!"

ABOUT THE AUTHOR

Ernie Carwile was born in Munich, Germany and has lived throughout the world. He is a graduate of the University of Missouri and the Iliff School of Theology in Denver, Colorado.

After high school he sold cemetery plots door-to-door in Hannibal, Missouri, and while attending college, he drove one of the huge trucks for Peabody Coal Mine. Mr. Carwile has been an Air force Officer, heavyweight boxer and a Methodist and Congregational minister.

As a celebrated author and master story-teller, Carwile has been featured extensively in the national media including *Good Morning America, Inside Edition, CNN,* the *Associated Press, Court TV, Clear Channel Radio,* the *Los Angeles Times* and the *Rocky Mountain News.*

His books have received a great review from the most prestigious *Library Journal,* as well as

Endorsements/Thank Yous from the President of the United States, twelve U.S. Governors and such prominent collegiate football coaches as Steve Spurrier. They also have been translated into five foreign languages.

Read the **Maxwell Winston Stone** Series
Books For Life!

www.ingramcontent.com/pod-product-compliance
Lightning Source LLC
Chambersburg PA
CBHW072144270326
41931CB00010B/1880